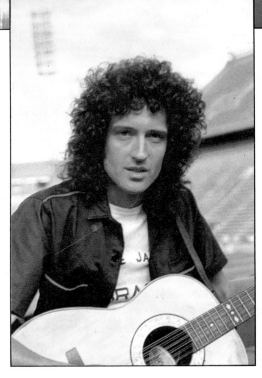

QUEEN

GREATEST HITS

PIANO · VOCAL · GUITAR

Editor Cecil Bolton
© 1981 EMI Music Publishing Ltd
International Music Publications Limited
Griffin House, 161 Hammersmith Road, London W6 8BS, England
Photographs: Neal Preston, Tony Frank/Sigma and Chris Hopper

Bohemian Rhapsody

Words and Music by FREDDIE MERCURY

8

12

no, no, no. Oh ma-ma mi-a, ma-ma mi-a. Ma-ma mi-a, let me go. Be-

Gb   Bb   Eb No chord   Eb   Bb

el - ze - bub has a dev - il put a - side for me,   for me, _____ for

Eb   Ab   D   Gm   Bb

me. _____

Instrumental Solo

Eb

So   you think you can stone me   and **spit in** my

F7   Bb7   Eb   Bb   Eb
                            (Bb bass)

14

Slowly, a tempo

Killer Queen

Words and Music by FREDDIE MERCURY

16

18

Another One Bites The Dust

Words and Music by JOHN DEACON

22

Fat Bottomed Girls

Words and Music by BRIAN MAY

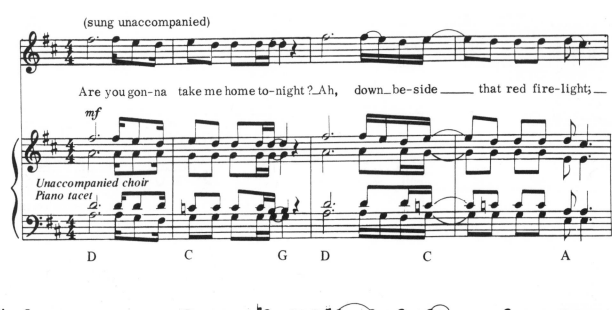

(sung unaccompanied)

Are you gon-na take me home to-night? Ah, down be-side that red fire-light;

D   C   G   D   C   A

are you gon-na let it all hang out? Fat bot-tomed girls, you make the rock-in' world go

D   G   D   A   Asus

Heavy Rock Beat

round. (Shout:) Hey! (Sing:) I was

(play) f

D

just a skin-ny lad nev-er knew___ no good from bad.___ But I knew
2. sing-ing with my band a-cross the wire,___ a-cross the land,___ I seen
3. mort-a-ges and homes, and the stiff-ness in your bones.___ Ain't no

D

life be-fore_ I left my nurs-er-y, Left a-lone___ with big fat Fan-ny, she was
ev-'ry blue_eyed floo-zy on the way. But their beau-ty and their style went kind of
beau-ty queens_ in this lo-cal-i-ty. (I tell you)Oh, but I___ still get my plea-sure still

A   D

such a naugh-ty nan-ny. Heap big wom-an you made a bad boy out of me.___
smooth af-ter a-while.___ Take me to them dirt-y la-dies ev-'ry-time.___
got my great-est trea-sure. Heap big wom-an you gon-na make a big man out of me._

1.

G   D   A   D

26

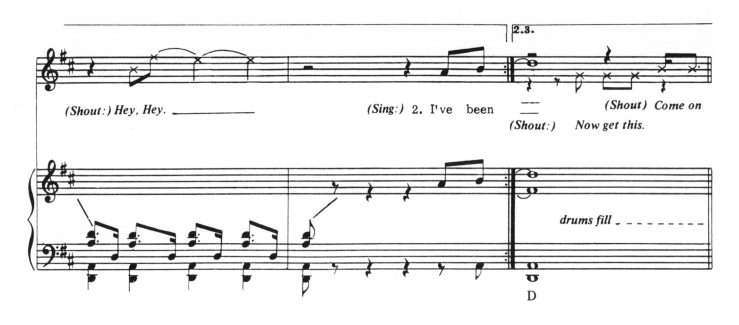

(Shout:) *Hey, Hey.* _____

(Sing:) 2. I've been

(Shout:) *Now get this.*

(Shout) *Come on*

drums fill _ _ _ _ _ _ _ _

D

chorus:

(Sing) Oh,   won't you   take   me   home   to - night?_
(Sing) Oh,   you gon - na   take   me   home   to - night. _ *(please)*

C   G

Oh,   down be-side__ your red   fire - light.__   Oh,   and   you
Oh,   down be-side__ your red   fire - light.__   Oh,   you gon - na

D   C   A   D

Bicycle Race

Words and Music by FREDDIE MERCURY

want to ___ ride my ___ bi - cy - cle, I want to ___ ride it ___

B♭m   A♭   B♭m

where I ___ like. You say black,   I say white, you say bark,   I say bite. You say shark,
                   I say caine, you say John,   I say Wayne. Hot   dog

A♭   B♭m

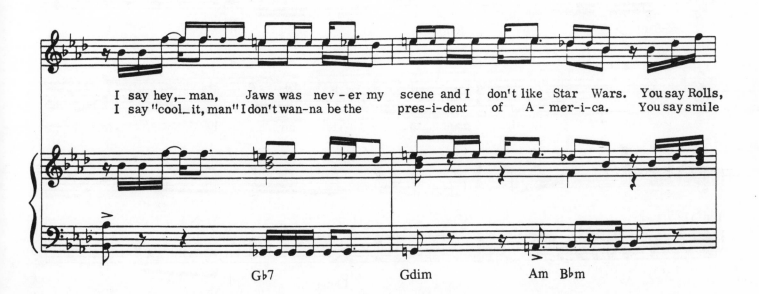

I say hey, ___ man, Jaws was nev - er my   scene and I   don't like Star Wars. You say Rolls,
I say "cool ___ it, man" I don't wan-na be the   pres-i-dent   of A - mer-i-ca.   You say smile

G♭7   Gdim   Am B♭m

31

32

You're My Best Friend

Words and Music by JOHN DEACON

Don't Stop Me Now

Words and Music by FREDDIE MERCURY

To Coda II

D.S. al Coda *Coda*

don't want to stop at all._____ I'm a

C7 Eb

N.C.

Don't stop me, don't stop me, don't stop me. Don't

stop me, don't stop me, ooh,___ ooh, ooh,___ Don't stop me, don't stop me, have a

Coda II

D.S. al Coda II *D.S.S. & fade*

good time, good time. Don't stop me, don't stop me. Ah! _____
(spoken)

Eb

Save Me

Words and Music by BRIAN MAY

Crazy Little Thing Called Love

Medium shuffle beat

Words and Music by FREDDIE MERCURY

(This thing) called love__ (called love) it cries__ (like a ba-by) in a

cra-dle all night,__ it swings__ (woo woo) it jives__ (woo woo) it

shakes all o-ver like a jel-ly fish,__ I kind-a like it

Cra-zy lit-tle thing called love.__ There goes my

48

Somebody To Love

Words and Music by FREDDIE MERCURY

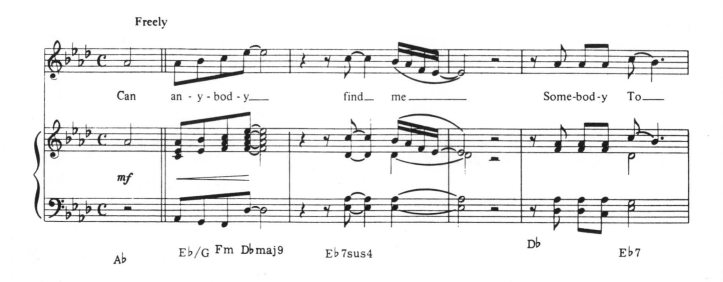

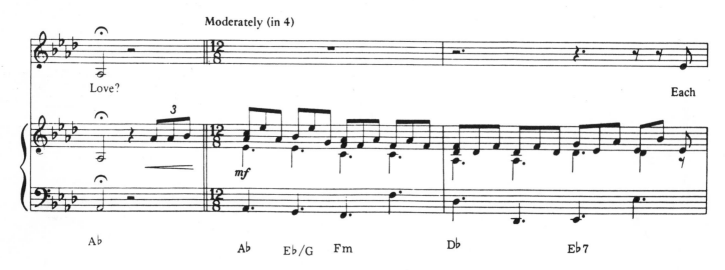

54

Find me some-bod-y to love,___ Find me some-bod-y to love,___

Ab

Find me some-bod-y to love,___ Find me some-bod-y to love,___

Find me some-bod-y to love.___ Find me some-bod-y to love,___

Find me some-bod-y to love,___ Some-bod-y, some-bod-y, some-bod-y, some-bod-y.

Good Old-Fashioned Lover Boy

Words and Music by FREDDIE MERCURY

60

love you.___ Hey boy, where did you get___ it from? Hey boy, where did you go?___ I

Bb7　　C7　　　　Fm

learned my pas - sion in the good old - fash - ioned school of lov - er

Abm　　　　　　　Bb7

boy.

Instrumental Solo

Eb　　Bb (D Bass)　　Cm　　Gm　Ab　　Eb　　Bb (D Bass)　　Cm　　G (B Bass)

D. C. al Fine

Cm　G　Cm　Gm　Fm　Ab　　Gm　Abm　　Eb Bb (D Bass)　Cm　Gm　　Fm　Abm　Bb7

Flash

Words and Music by BRIAN MAY

66

Seven Seas Of Rhye

Words and Music by FREDDIE MERCURY

Repeat ad lib for fade

Play The Game

Words and Music by FREDDIE MERCURY

1. Op-en up your mind and let me step in-side.
2. When you're feel-in' down and your re-sis-tance is low.
3. Instrumental

Rest your wear-y head and let your heart de-cide. It's so ea-sy,
Light an-oth-er ci-ga-rette and let your-self go. This is your life,

when you know the rules. It's so ea-sy, all you have to do is fall in love
don't play hard to get. It's a free world, all you have to do is fall in love

72

We Will Rock You

Words and Music by BRIAN MAY

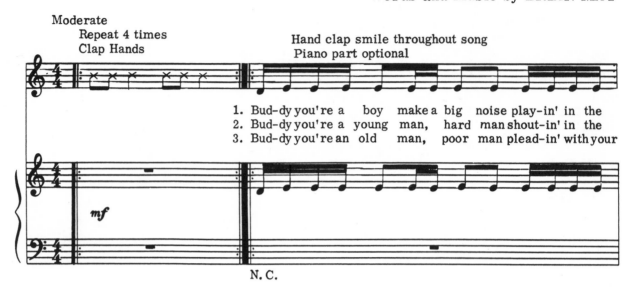

3.

We will we will rock you   We will we will rock you.   We will we will

rock you.

C   A   D   A

D   A   Asus   D   A   Asus

Play 3 times

A

Now I'm Here

Words and Music by BRIAN MAY

78

We Are The Champions

Words and Music by FREDDIE MERCURY

84